STARTING YOUR OWN BUSINESS

CECILIA MINDEN

Published in the United States of America by Cherry Lake Publishing
Ann Arbor, Michigan
www.cherrylakepublishing.com

Math Education: Dr. Timothy Whiteford, Associate Professor of Education at St. Michael's College
Financial Adviser: Kenneth Klooster, financial adviser at Edward Jones Investments
Reading Adviser: Marla Conn, ReadAbility, Inc.

Photo Credits: © Maxirf | Dreamstime.com, cover, 1, 28; © ChameleonsEye/Shutterstock Images, 5; © AVAVA/ Shutterstock Images, 6; © Jakub Zak/Shutterstock Images, 9; © SpeedKingz/Shutterstock Images, 10; © Monkey Business Images/Shutterstock Images, 12, 23; © Davis Sacks/Thinkstock.com, 15; © Picsfive/Shutterstock Images, 16; © David Kam Photography/Thinkstock.com, 19; © Jami Garrison/Thinkstock.com, 21; © Jorge Salcedo/Shutterstock Images, 24; © izustun/Thinkstock.com, 27

Library of Congress Cataloging-in-Publication Data

Minden, Cecilia.
     Starting your own business / Cecilia Minden.
     pages cm. — (Real world math: personal finance)
     Includes bibliographical references and index.
     ISBN 978-1-63362-576-1 (hardcover) — ISBN 978-1-63362-756-7 (pdf) —
     ISBN 978-1-63362-666-9 (pbk.) — ISBN 978-1-63362-846-5 (ebook)
     1. New business enterprises—Juvenile literature. 2. Entrepreneurship—Juvenile literature. 3. Small business—Management—Juvenile literature. 4. Business mathematics—Juvenile literature. I. Title.

     HD62.5.M548 2016
     658.1'1—dc23   2015008970

Cherry Lake Publishing would like to acknowledge the work of
the Partnership for 21st Century Skills. Please visit www.p21.org
for more information.

Printed in the United States of America
Corporate Graphics

ABOUT THE AUTHOR

Cecilia Minden, PhD, is a former classroom teacher and university professor. She now enjoys working as a literacy consultant and writer for school and library publications. She has written more than 50 books for children. Cecilia started her first business in the third grade, selling homemade crafts to her kind and generous family.

TABLE OF CONTENTS

CHAPTER 1

It Starts With a Great Idea

Mark Zuckerberg was a student at Harvard when he had an idea for a student Web site. Ben Cohen and Jerry Greenfield were childhood friends who took a course in making ice cream. Emilie Legrand and Christina Ha loved cookies and cats.

Each of these **entrepreneurs** saw a need, and all of them formed their ideas into successful businesses. Zuckerberg created Facebook. Ben and Jerry became "Ben & Jerry" and created "Vermont's Finest" ice cream. Legrand and Ha opened Meow Parlour, a New York City bakery where you can munch cookies and cuddle cats.

Ben & Jerry's has grown into a very successful brand of ice cream.

Would you like to turn your ideas into a successful business? First, you need to understand how a business works.

There are five basic steps to follow in creating your own business:

- Have an idea.
- Create a business plan.
- Fund your idea.
- Market your product.
- Manage your business.

If you have a passion for sewing, you can try to use that skill for a new business.

Step 1: Have an idea. Where do you get an idea to create a business? Begin with what you know. How do you like to spend your time? What activity makes you happy? What are your passions and talents? Brainstorm ideas with others. Keep an ongoing list of possibilities.

Caring for a younger sibling will teach you how to care for small children. This could lead to your own babysitting service. Helping to care for Grandma's yard could lead to your own lawn care company. Maybe you have skills in baking, sewing, computers, or sports.

Once you have several ideas, narrow them down to ideas you can sell to others.

Use your math skills to create a chart or graph. Highlight the strengths and weaknesses of each idea. Test your ideas with people you trust to give you an honest opinion. Once you decide, you will need a business plan. Math plays an important role in getting your business off to a great start.

REAL WORLD MATH CHALLENGE

Sophie has a business making dog blankets. Each blanket requires $3.85 worth of materials. She pays her little sister $4.00 an hour to help her. Together, they can make 3 blankets in an hour.

- How much will Sophie need to charge per blanket to make $3.00 on each of the 3 blankets?

(Turn to page 30 for the answers)

CHAPTER 2

WRITING A BUSINESS PLAN

Step 2: Create a business plan. Think of the business plan as the bone structure of your company. Without bones, your body would collapse. Without a good business plan, your company will do the same.

A business plan should answer who, what, how, where, and why questions about your business. It should include:

- business concept
- company description
- service or product description

Every great business starts with a good, well-written business plan.

- understanding of the **market**
- description of **finances**

Let's explore what each of these means and how each one is important to your business.

The *business concept* is a written statement explaining your business. The explanation should accurately describe your goals. Give reasons why you are qualified to produce these goods or provide these services. The *company description* explains what you will be doing. It should highlight the company's goals and objectives. Are you

Try asking a local business owner for advice on how to get started.

21ST CENTURY CONTENT

The U.S. Small Business Administration (SBA) helps small business owners and protects their interests. The SBA's mission is to help "Americans start, build and grow businesses." Do you shop at a locally owned business? Talk to the owner about what it is like to own your own business.

LIFE AND CAREER SKILLS

Use your computer skills to see what other students are doing to earn money. Research business plans written by other students. Learn from others as you are creating your business.

going to do all the work? Maybe you plan to hire a couple of friends to help you. Be sure to include where your business will be located.

The *service or product description* should briefly explain what you are selling. How are you going to make this product or provide this service? Include photographs or drawings to help others visualize what you plan to do. Spend time with each section of the plan until you are confident it accurately represents your product or service.

You can't sell what others aren't buying. For example,

There's a market for snow shoveling in the winter, but not usually in the spring, summer, or fall.

if everyone you know already has a school T-shirt, then don't start a business selling school T-shirts. There is no market for them. An *understanding of the market* helps you know if there is a need for your product or service. In this section, include why your business will meet and satisfy the needs of your customers.

The *description of finances* section of your business plan shows exactly how much it will cost to produce your product or service. How many products can you make/services can you do and in what amount of time?

Do you need to include helpers to reach your goals? What will that cost?

Prove you have a good idea by using your math skills to create a simple business plan. Take the time to think through ideas and research the facts. Now you are ready to share your idea with others.

REAL WORLD MATH CHALLENGE

Mia plans to offer dog-walking services to her neighbors this summer. She plans to walk 3 dogs per day and charge $10.00 per dog per day. But she can only walk one dog at a time, since the leashes get tangled up.

- If she walks 3 dogs per day, how many days of work will it take her to achieve her end-of-summer goal of earning $1,500.00?
- How many walks will Mia end up going on?

(Turn to page 30 for the answers)

Do the Math: Finding Investors

Step 3: Fund your idea. Starting a new business takes hard work and patience. When you have a great idea, it is natural to want to start working on it right away. First, you need the money to get the business going.

Begin with your own money. Having a business means making choices. You may need to put off a personal shopping trip and use the money for your business instead. One source of income is an allowance. Create a **budget** for your personal

A yard sale can be a good way to raise enough money to start your business.

expenses. Where can you save money for the business? Can you skip going to the movies or buying snacks at the mall? Having your own business means making a few sacrifices. Look for ways to earn other income while you work on getting your business started.

You may decide the best way to support your new business is to seek investors. An investor is someone who is willing to give you money to start your business. An investor may loan you the money or ask for a percentage of the **profits**. A loan is usually repaid with interest. This

A profit is the money you have left after you pay your business expenses.

means extra money is charged for borrowing the money. For example, you borrow $50.00 from Grandpa John to start a business. You agree to pay him $5.00 a week on the principal (which is the $50.00) plus 5 percent interest until the loan is paid off. The first week, you pay $5.00 plus 5 percent of $50.00, or $2.50. The total payment is $7.50. The next week, the principal is now $45.00, so you pay $5.00 plus 5 percent of $45.00, or $2.25, for a total of $7.25. The payments continue until the loan is paid off.

Other investors receive money from a **share** of the profits. Let's say you decide to keep 60 percent of the profits for yourself. You sell shares to investors and use the money to start the business. Four people each buy a 10 percent share in your company. This means that after expenses are paid, you owe each investor 10 percent of the profits. If your business is doing well, the investors could earn more than their original investment. It is a chance investors are willing to take for a product they think will do well. They keep earning 10 percent of the profits until they sell their shares back to you or to someone else.

LIFE AND CAREER SKILLS

A good way to learn together is to form a business club at school or on your own. Invite successful business owners to share their ideas with you.

Use your math skills to decide which type of investor you need for your company. Remember, the best way to get investors is to have a good business plan they can read. A business plan will tell them about your company and help them understand your goals.

REAL WORLD MATH CHALLENGE

Eduardo wants to start a lawn-mowing business, but he needs to buy a lawn mower. The one he wants costs $237.44 including tax. He doesn't have any money to buy the lawn mower, but he has 4 people willing to invest in his company.

- How much will he need to get from each investor to buy the lawn mower?

He agrees to pay back each loan with 5 percent interest at the end of the summer.

- How much will he pay each investor?

(Turn to page 30 for the answers)

Mowing lawns can be a good way to make money during the summer.

CHAPTER 4

Do the Math: Marketing

Step 4: Market your product. You have an idea, a plan, and investors. How do you get your product or service out to the public? You market your product. There are two kinds of marketing. *Inbound marketing* is all about making sure you meet the needs of your current customers. What can you do to keep them as your customers? People always have a choice. What makes your business the one they should continue to use?

Outbound marketing is getting information about your product or service out to other customers. To do this, you would use advertisements or promotions.

A flyer is one way to advertise, especially if you are skilled on the computer. Are you selling a product? Be sure you include all the information a customer would

You might post an ad on social media, where everyone you know can see it.

REAL WORLD MATH CHALLENGE

Gabriel is starting a business to help senior citizens set up their home computers. His research showed that most of his **potential** customers read the local newspaper. He has $400.00 budgeted for advertising. The cost of a local newspaper ad is $150.00 for a small ad.

- How many days can his ad appear in the newspaper?
- How much more money does he need to run the ad another day?

(Turn to page 30 for the answers)

need to understand your product or service. Begin by including your name and the name of your business. How will customers contact you? Talk to your parents before giving out a home phone number or personal e-mail address. Decorate the flyer with photographs or drawings of your product or service. Do you have a catchy phrase or slogan you can use on the flyer? Experiment with different slogans until you come up with one you think people will remember.

Share your flyer with a few people before you print

In some communities, there's a demand for teaching senior citizens how to use the most modern technology.

Some places advertise by putting ads on top of cars.

out many copies. Get some feedback. Is the flyer easy to understand? Does it have all the information? Did you use correct grammar and spelling? You want to make a good first impression with the people who may become your customers!

Another way to market your product is with a special promotion. A typical supermarket promotion is buy one, get one free. Maybe you could sell three products for the price of two, to first-time customers. Another promotion might be giving out a small gift card to a local restaurant with each purchase of a certain amount.

Another way to promote your business is by using your own products—leading by example. For example, you could wear samples from your jewelry-making business.

The best marketing tool for your business is your reputation. Give prompt and courteous service. Take the time to do good work. The extra care will pay off when your customers recommend you to their friends.

21ST CENTURY CONTENT

Advertising is a major part of big businesses. TV ads during the Super Bowl are among the most expensive. A 30-second ad costs millions of dollars. The ad has to catch the viewer's attention and sell the product. Advertisers use humor, suspense, and big stars. Why do you think big companies are willing to spend so much on a single ad during the Super Bowl?

CHAPTER 5

MANAGING A SUCCESSFUL BUSINESS

Step 5: Manage your business. Doing this successfully means knowing how to handle different people and situations. In addition, you want to keep your customers satisfied, but you can't let the business run your life.

You still need to eat, go to school, get plenty of rest, and have fun with family and friends. How will you find time for a business? The key is time management. This means you know how to balance your time between things you need to do and things you want to do.

For a couple weeks, write down what you do and how

To-do lists can be useful tools to help you manage your priorities.

much time it takes you to do it. Now add in the time it will take to run your business. Be realistic, and don't forget transportation time to and from activities. Setting priorities means doing what needs to be done first. Then you can do what you want to do. Never make your customers promises that you can't keep. If you don't have time to do the work for them now, try to find another day when you can take care of their needs. Setting priorities helps you find time for everything without falling behind.

If you love taking care of animals, walking dogs might be a great business idea for you.

21ST CENTURY CONTENT

Junior Achievement is the "world's largest organization dedicated to educating students about work readiness, entrepreneurship and financial literacy through experiential, hands-on programs." Around the globe, more than 8 million students take part in business competitions each year. Participating in these competitions can be a good way to learn to work with others. Is there a Junior Achievement organization in your community?

Another priority for business is safety. Always be sure you are working where you will not cause harm to yourself or anyone else. This is especially true when caring for children or pets. You are responsible not only for your safety but for theirs as well.

Ready to get your own business up and running? You just might end up using your math skills in another way—adding up your profits!

REAL WORLD MATH CHALLENGE

Isabella and Rosie started a business making fancy cupcakes for children's parties. Mrs. Watts ordered 36 cupcakes for her daughter's party. Baking supplies and cupcake papers totaled $17.89 with tax. Isabella's mother allowed them to use her kitchen if they promised to clean up afterward.

- How much will each cupcake cost?
- How much will the girls need to charge so that each of them earns $0.75 for each cupcake?
- How much should they charge Mrs. Watts for 36 cupcakes?

(Turn to page 30 for the answers)

REAL WORLD MATH CHALLENGE ANSWERS

CHAPTER ONE
Page 7

Sophie must charge $8.18 for each blanket to make a $3.00 profit.
$3.85 for materials x 3 blankets = $11.55 for the cost of materials per hour
$11.55 + $4.00 per hour to pay her sister = $15.55 in total costs per hour
$15.55 ÷ 3 blankets = $5.18 for each blanket with no profit
$5.18 + $3.00 profit = $8.18

CHAPTER TWO
Page 13

Mia will have to work 50 days to reach her goal of $1,500.00.
$10.00 per dog x 3 dogs per day = $30.00 earned each day
$1,500.00 goal ÷ $30.00 = 50 days

She will end up going on 150 walks.
50 days x 3 dogs per day = 150

CHAPTER THREE
Page 18

Eduardo will need $59.36 from each investor.
$237.44 for the lawn mower ÷ 4 investors = $59.36

Each investor will receive $62.33.
$59.36 x 0.05 interest = $2.97 (rounded up from $2.968)
$2.97 + $59.36 = $62.33

CHAPTER FOUR
Page 22

Gabriel's ad can run for 2 days.
$400.00 budgeted ÷ $150.00 for a small ad = 2 days, with $100.00 remaining

He needs $50 .00 more to run the ad for 1 more day.
$150.00 − $100.00 = $50.00

CHAPTER FIVE
Page 29

The cost of each cupcake is about $0.50.
$17.89 ÷ 36 cupcakes = $0.50 per cupcake (rounded up from $0.4969)

Isabella and Rosie should charge $2.00 per cupcake.
$0.75 x 2 = $1.50 profit for both girls per cupcake
$1.50 + $0.50 = $2.00

They should charge Mrs. Watts $72.00 for the cupcakes.
36 cupcakes x $2.00 = $72.00

FIND OUT MORE

BOOKS

Bernstein, Daryl. *Better Than a Lemonade Stand!: Small Business Ideas for Kids.* New York: Aladdin/Beyond Words; Reissue Edition, 2012.

Jacobson, Ryan, and Jon Cannell (Illustrator). *Get a Job Helping Others.* Minneapolis: Lerner Publishing Group, 2014.

WEB SITES

Junior Achievement
https://www.juniorachievement.org/web/ja-usa/home
Learn about the organization and how it trains young entrepreneurs.

TeachingKidsBusiness.com
www.teachingkidsbusiness.com/how-to-start-your-own-business.htm
Discover various resources to help get your business started.

GLOSSARY

budget (BUHJ-it) a plan for how money will be earned, spent, and saved

entrepreneurs (ahn-truh-pruh-NURZ) people who start new businesses

finances (FYE-nans-iz) the amount of money a business or individual has and how it is managed

market (MAHR-kit) possible demand for certain goods or services

potential (puh-TEN-shuhl) possible but not yet actual or real

profits (PRAH-fits) money that is left after business expenses are paid

share (SHAIR) ownership portion of a company

INDEX